Deborah Griffin first blessed the lives of the members of the church I pastor, and my life, as a member of our church leadership team and an exemplary, godly single parent. Now she is poised to bless the entire body of Christ through her excellent book, *Single for a Season, Married for a Reason*. She skillfully weaves personal testimony, prose, poetry, and Scripture into a beautiful tapestry of inspiration, counsel, and guidance for the single Christian, while calling her readers to a life of total commitment to Christ. A must-read!

—CHARLES H. WILLIAMS
PASTOR, GRACE CHAPEL
INGLEWOOD, CALIFORNIA

single
for a
season
married
for a
reason

Deborah Griffin

CREATION HOUSE

SINGLE FOR A SEASON, MARRIED FOR A REASON
by Deborah Griffin
Published by Creation House
A Strang Company
600 Rinehart Road
Lake Mary, Florida 32746
www.creationhouse.com

Unless otherwise noted, all Scripture quotations are from the New King James Version of the Bible. Copyright © 1979, 1980, 1982 by Thomas Nelson, Inc., publishers. Used by permission.

Scripture quotations marked KJV are from the King James Version of the Bible.

Cover design by Rachel Campbell

Library of Congress Control Number: 2006936889
International Standard Book Number-10: 1-59979-092-0
International Standard Book Number-13: 978-1-59979-092-3

First Edition

07 08 09 10 — 987654321
Printed in the United States of America

Contents

Acknowledgments

- My heartfelt "thank you" to my daughter, Nicole, for your patient and tolerant spirit during the many hours I spent harkening to the leading of the Holy Spirit while writing this book.

- And a gracious "thank you" to a humble man of God, Pastor Charles Williams (Grace Chapel in Inglewood, California), for your candid and prompt input and pastoral guidance.

- A special note of "thanks" goes out to all my family members and friends. Your endless encouragement, support, and belief in me, over the years, propelled me to this time and place. And look what the Lord has done!

Introduction

THE JOURNEY WE'RE about to take together will be absolutely life changing! If you are single with a desire to one day marry, stay tuned! I'm about to share some of the most God-inspired, supernatural insights put on my heart to touch countless lives. Your life will be touched and you will be blessed!

And even if you're not single, you will be blessed too! Perhaps you need restoration in your marriage or other relationships. This book reaches beyond the community of "singles." There is an underlying message for the *church* and every individual on planet Earth that is searching for a better life, a better future, and more importantly, an eternal promise!

Many of the principles we'll examine apply to *singles* or couples. Let's be transformed together as we move in God's anointed Word. Open your heart and expect to be taken to a new level of completeness, wholeness, and purpose!

Please speak the following prayer out loud and believe.

The words you are about to declare have *power*. Jesus, in His infinite wisdom, knew the day you would release this prayer into the atmosphere. He is watching and waiting…just believe!

Heavenly Father, I thank You for Your Word. You said that You watch over Your Word to perform it and that Your Word does not return to You void. Give me wisdom and understanding to receive those things that You will deposit into my heart. Give me ears to hear what the Spirit says. Anoint me to receive fresh revelation from above and establish it in my life.

Lord, I thank You for the genuine love You have for me. I declare that the same love You have for me is what I want to see manifested in me and in my relationships with others. Lord Jesus, increase my territory and faith so that I can move beyond what I see in the natural realm. I decree and declare that the supernatural seed (Word) You are about to plant in my heart will take root and produce a bountiful harvest. And out of the abundance, I will speak life into others around me. My eyes are open, my ears are open, my heart is open, and I'm ready to receive Your truth…and the truth will make me free! I'm expecting to hear from You, Lord!

Now Father, I thank You in advance for the transformation that will take place. By faith, I'm confessing that You are going to bring me to a place where Your glory will penetrate every area of my life. I lift my hands in Your presence and decree and declare that what You are getting ready to do in my life is not by my might or power but by the Spirit of the living God. Amen!

One *Single* Journey

We're about to journey to a place called truth
First let's go back to the time of our youth
No worries, no cares, no bills to pay
The stresses of life were not part of your day
Our hearts were pure enough to believe
Our minds seemed more open to receive
This is how God created us to be
He wanted that peace for you and for me
But then we traveled into another land
We soon lost sight of God's outstretched hand
And ever since, He's been calling us back
His only desire, to restore what we lack
When we voyage through life with the *One*
    on the throne
Even in our *singleness*, we're never alone.

—Deborah J. Griffin

Chapter 1

A Few *Single* Things We've Missed

I REMEMBER READING A book years ago that contained good insight into living single and rejoicing in "singleness." Trust me, I had heard it before: "When you are single, you have the perfect opportunity to totally set yourself apart to the Lord without the distractions marriage brings." This is true, but at that point in my life, I was not there. I was not ready to receive it. I wanted a man in the flesh—I wanted to be married! Listen, I'm being honest! And I believe the reason the Lord has "singled" me out to be His voice is because there will be many single women reading this book who feel exactly like I felt. If you are one of those women, keep reading! *I have good news for you!* And if you're not, praise God! But keep on reading anyhow; God has something for you too!

Now for all the single men out there: Don't you miss out on what God is saying! This book is for you too!

I'll begin by addressing those who are challenged with living this life we call "single." And just so you're aware, I'm speaking primarily to the group we call the "body of Christ." But even if you don't have a relationship with Jesus and you're searching, this is for you too. The Lord is waiting to take you to a place where you truly can enjoy your "singleness." As a matter of fact, I'm going to be bold enough to say that what you're about to read will allow you to "delight yourself also in the LORD" (Ps. 37:4), like never before. You will reach a level of intimacy that, especially in your singleness, will be incredible. It will happen, and you will be amazed. And as His Word declares, if your true desire is for a mate, God will give you the desire of your heart in His perfect timing (see Ps. 37:4).

Expect the Lord to transport you into the fullness that only He can bring. He will do it while you are *single*. Let's begin the journey together. Let's receive His promise together!

Don't Miss a *Single* Blessing!

It is amazing how many blessings we miss because we are unwilling to go through a few trials. Consider the horrific sacrifice our Lord and Savior, Jesus Christ, made on our behalf as He was mocked, beaten, bruised, nailed to the cross, pierced in His side, and totally separated from God. Now that, my friend, is a trial! If we were to seriously take the time to reflect on the excruciating pain Christ endured, it would give new meaning to "My yoke is easy and My burden is light" (Matt. 11:30). How often do we magnify the trials and tests we face? I'm not making light of those things that can truly paralyze us for a season in life. But all too often, the things that come against us are miniscule when compared to the suffering of our Lord Jesus Christ. We need to be more mindful of how we handle and view our obstacles. When we are tested beyond our capacity to stand, God's grace is sufficient if we believe. His desire is to bring us through each and every one of life's disappointments victoriously, and in the process, He does not want us to miss a *single* blessing!

God wants to bless us. He wants us to prosper in all areas of our lives. The Word of God declares:

> Beloved, I pray that you may prosper in all things
> and be in health, just as your soul prospers.
> —3 JOHN 1:2

The Book of Job tells us of one man's true pain and suffering. Job lost everything—his property, children, and ultimately his health (see Job 1:13–21; 2:7–8). Job is probably one of the most heartfelt books in the Bible that is packed with lessons on dealing with loss. The true lesson that God ultimately reveals is His desire to bless. The story ends with Job's complete restoration. In the end, Job is blessed with twice as much as he had before everything was taken from him (see Job 42:12–13). But there was some instruction Job had to receive from the Lord before the restoration took place (see Job 38–42). God allows each one of us, just like Job, to experience loss so that we will come to recognize His sovereign control in *all* things in our lives. Even in the midst of our pain and suffering, we need to surrender to God and believe He is for us and not against us. Let us never forget God's promise:

> I have come that they may have life, and that they may have it more abundantly.
>
> —JOHN 10:10

There will be trials; there will be tests. But with the right heart, attitude, and mind towards God, you will never miss a *single* blessing He has for you!

DON'T *SINGLE* ME OUT!

Somehow we have allowed the truth to be distorted, and a myth exists today that says, "Because of your *singleness,* you are incomplete." That, my friend, is a lie from the pit of hell. Nothing can be further from the truth. Let's take a look at how the Word of God addresses this matter.

Paul, an apostle of Jesus Christ, wrote in his letter to the church of Corinth:

> But I say to the unmarried and to the widows: It is good for them if they remain even as I am; but if they cannot exercise self-control, let them marry.
>
> —1 CORINTHIANS 7:8–9

Another scripture that confronts this myth is:

> The unmarried woman cares about the things of the Lord…But she who is married cares about the things

of the world—how she may please her husband.
—1 CORINTHIANS 7:34

That is not to say God does not want us to marry. Marriage is spoken of all throughout the Bible. Christ Himself makes a profound comparison between the institution of marriage and the church.

For the husband is head of the wife, as also Christ is head of the church.

—EPHESIANS 5:23

He who finds a wife finds a good thing, And obtains favor from the LORD.

—PROVERBS 18:22

God wants us to be complete while we are single, so that if and when we do marry, He is able to bring us into a relationship that is "whole." Do not let anyone *single* you out and say you are incomplete unless you are married. Nowhere in the Bible does it speak of this. God has a purpose and a plan for your life that goes way beyond who you do (or do not) marry. Jeremiah 29:11 says, "For I know the thoughts that I think toward you, says the LORD."

There are many single men and women in the Bible that were used mightily of God. Look at Paul the Apostle, who, under the inspiration of the Holy Spirit, wrote most of the New Testament recorded in the Holy Bible. Most people are familiar with the story of Esther. She played a monumental role in the deliverance of many from certain death. There are so many other examples. Read your Bible for yourself and you will be amazed. I am still reading, I am still learning, and I am still fascinated! Don't let your singleness prevent God from using you. He can use you mightily. Don't ever forget that!

God Will Perfect You
Single-Handedly—Just Be Patient!

Most of us are unwilling to patiently wait for the Lord to perfect us and (ultimately) give us more than we could ever imagine. Instead, we devise our own plans that, in most cases, are totally unsuccessful. In the end, we waste more time than it would have taken if we had simply, patiently waited on the Lord.

A personal word that God has given me for 2006 is this: "Be still, and know that I am God" (Ps. 46:10). I often meditate on this scripture as Christ brings it to my remembrance. One of my struggles throughout life has been my inability to be patient. I'm still not quite where I should be, but God has brought me a long way. When we are far enough along in our relationship with God to hear His voice, He begins to speak to us about those secret things, such as the promises that have been stored up for us before the foundation of the world. God is just waiting to release His promises to you. Yes, you! He wants you to step out in faith and believe. He will not disappoint you. His Word is true.

> Therefore it is of faith that it might be according to grace, so that the promise might be sure to all the seed.
>
> —Romans 4:16

If we are sons and daughters of God, we are His seed. God is always speaking to us, but many of us miss Him because of all the distractions around us. We need to be still, and we need to be patient.

You may be thinking, *Debbie, you just have not been where I've been. You have not walked in my shoes. There's no way you can understand my pain, my loneliness.* You're right! I don't know, and I probably will never understand, but God does! Is there anything too difficult for Him? Absolutely not! One thing I do know is that in my singleness, there have been times I've cried myself to sleep at night, wishing to be held and comforted, feeling alone and rejected, used and abused, longing for companionship, and longing to be loved. So, my sisters and brothers, I do feel some of your pain. Jesus is the answer!

> Be anxious for nothing, but in everything by prayer and supplication, with thanksgiving, let your requests be made known to God; and the peace of God, which surpasses all understanding, will guard your hearts and minds through Christ Jesus.
> —PHILIPPIANS 4:6–7

> Rest in the LORD, and wait patiently for Him.
> —PSALM 37:7

These scriptures changed my life when they became real to me. You need to get real with God. Tell Him about your pain, your loneliness, or whatever it is you are carrying. Release your cares and burdens to God!

His Word, in 1 Peter 5:7, tells us to: "[Cast] all your care upon Him, for He cares for you." Allow Him to comfort you. He will give you peace, joy, and victory. If it is your desire to marry, I believe God will bring it to pass. My question to you is, Will you allow Him to bring it to pass?

Let God restore, heal, and perfect you while you are single. God holds all power in His hand and He can perfect you single-handedly. Just be patient!

Always remember:

> He who has begun a good work in you will complete it.
>
> —PHILIPPIANS 1:6

BE HONEST WITH GOD. HE KNOWS EVERY *SINGLE* THING ANYWAY!

There was a time in my life when I was in relationship after relationship. I experienced many years of unnecessary hurt, pain, confusion, and delusion. I was like the woman at the well. You probably remember the story as told in the Book of John (chapter 4).

When Jesus was passing through the city of Samaria, He met a woman at the well and asked her to give Him a drink. As they continued conversing, Jesus said to her:

> "Go, call your husband..." The woman answered and said, "I have no husband." Jesus said to her, "You have well said, 'I have no husband,' for you have had five husbands, and the one whom you now have is

8

not your husband; *in that you spoke truly.*"
—JOHN 4:16–18, EMPHASIS ADDED

Here was an unmarried woman (after having five husbands), who was in a relationship with yet another man, who was not her husband. Yet, even in her circumstance, Jesus commended her for her honesty. If you've been there (or are there), the first step is to be honest with God. He knows where you've been and how long you've been there, and He's waiting to offer you the real "living water" that will satisfy whatever it is that is causing you to keep "dipping into that well." He did it for me and He will do it for you! If I had been the woman at that well, the number would have been much greater than five. However, God has forgiven me and He will forgive you too.

Be honest with God, ask for forgiveness, and move on. He knows every single thing anyway!

> O LORD, You have searched me and known me. You know my sitting down and my rising up; You understand my thought afar off. You comprehend my path and my lying down, And are acquainted with all my ways. For there is not a word on my tongue, But behold, O LORD, You know it altogether. You have hedged me behind and before, And laid Your hand upon me. Such knowledge is too wonderful for me; It is high, I cannot attain it. Where can I go from Your Spirit? Or where can I flee from Your presence? If I ascend into heaven, You are there; If I make my bed in hell, behold, You are there.
> —PSALM 139:1–8

ARE YOU *SINGLE*- OR DOUBLE-MINDED?

Do you not know that when you join yourself to another human being, you become one flesh? Jesus tells us of God's original design for mankind:

> Have you not read that He who made them at the beginning "made them male and female,"…and the two shall become one flesh.
>
> —MATTHEW 19:4–5

The Lord began to reveal to me that there are many single people walking around with double minds. It is because they are carrying around "fleshly" sediments and ashes that they inherited from joining themselves to other individuals outside of marriage. As a matter of fact, there are many single people walking around with multiple minds—I was one of them. I am not telling you these things for you to slip into condemnation. Remember, we are seeking truth so we can be transformed and made single-minded and *whole!* The Lord calls us in James 4:8 to "purify your hearts, you double-minded." Having a single mind towards the things of Christ enables us to abstain from the lustful desires of the flesh that lure us into surrendering to an impure lifestyle.

God showed me how our double-mindedness causes us to waver back and forth. As a result, we're never able to put Him first and we end up being drawn to the lusts of the world. Our double-mindedness also keeps us from moving beyond our unstable ways, and therefore we keep going in opposite directions. This is a very uncomfortable place to live. This is why we lack discipline. *Again, this is why we lack discipline!*

Some may argue that in our singleness, we may occasionally lose sight of our true value and completeness. In reality, it is our double-mindedness that is perpetuating the emptiness or loneliness we may experience at times. I used to feel incomplete until I took hold of who I am in Christ Jesus and began to see myself as He sees me. I am truly the "apple of His eye" (Deut. 32:10). And guess what? So are you! Get excited and start expecting and receiving the love God has for you. And as an added bonus, enjoy His peace.

> You will keep him in perfect peace, Whose mind is stayed on You.
> —ISAIAH 26:3

IF THERE'S ONE *SINGLE* THING I'VE LEARNED, IT'S GOD'S FAVOR AND FORGIVENESS THAT EMPOWERS US TO LIVE HOLY!

Another truth Jesus revealed to me in Scripture comes from a familiar story that tells of the woman who was caught in the act of adultery. That's right, in the very act!

When her accusers brought her before Jesus, He responded by saying:

> He who is without sin among you, let him throw a stone at her first.
> —JOHN 8:7

Needless to say, Jesus and that woman were standing there alone within a very short period of time. And then Jesus looked at her and said:

> Woman, where are those accusers of yours? Has no one condemned you?…Neither do I condemn you; go and sin no more.
>
> —John 8:10–11

This is an awesome account of God's favor and resolve to forgive and empower us to live holy. I believe that if Jesus told that woman to sin no more, He empowered her to do it. And that power can work for you and me too! We do not have to be slaves to sin or slaves to lust. Let's stop making excuses and live right. I'm not saying we will never make a mistake, and when we do, God will forgive us. But we need to stop giving in to every fleshly desire…you know what I'm talking about. We need to start living holy. Don't get mad at me! God said:

> Be ye holy; for I am holy.
>
> —1 Peter:1:16, KJV

This is some good stuff! And I didn't do a *single* thing but listen to the prompting of the Holy Spirit to give you this awesome insight. And it's just the tip of the iceberg. As our journey continues, we will go deeper and deeper. God is *singling* you out to elevate you to a place of purity, joy, and peace in being *single for a season*!

Praise God! Take a deep breath and hold on to your

seat, because we are moving out of shallow water. We are going deeper!

SINGLE, SEXY, AND SAVED. HOLD ON TO YOUR SEAT!

When the Lord began to bring me to this topic, my immediate reaction was, *Jesus what are you doing?* His response to me was, "I am the Creator of all good things." Yes, God created sex, and it is good. But before I write another word, I want you to know that I partied with the best of them. I became the best of them. I have done things that would turn your head. If you knew me, you would probably be surprised, because I'm actually a very conservative person in many ways. But there's a little truth in that saying, "You can't judge a book by its cover." Can I be honest with you? It's time for someone to stand up, be real, and tell it like it is. Well, guess what? God is sending me, and I'm not ashamed to go. Even though I've missed it (BIG TIME) along the way, I have been forgiven of every *single* mistake I've made. Every *single* sin has been covered by the blood of Jesus. Now that we've established that I'm not here to judge or condemn anyone, let me tell you what God has put on my heart. And He's going to confirm it with His Word.

Now, I'm going to repeat what I said earlier: sex is good! Please bear with me for a few moments and I'll take you to another level of intimacy—what God originally created. Sadly, we have allowed the devil to distort what was meant for our pleasure and to use it as a weapon against us. People are dying! Wake up! Look at what is going on around us! Our children are being sexually molested at unprecedented levels, AIDS is killing thousands daily, and pornography has captivated our youth and has stirred up horrifying desires in the hearts of mankind. The number of sexually transmitted diseases permeating around the globe is astounding. All in the name of sex! This is not what God intended. Do not be deceived.

Please don't tune me out. Our healing—your healing—is so wrapped up in what God is about to speak through me. Just keep reading and hold on to your seat!

When God began to unveil His plan of intimacy for you and me, I began to weep over how far we have come from His original intention. Sex was supposed to be an ultimate expression of love. And from this gift, we were supposed to benefit by enjoying the most paramount expression of trust, commitment, unity, loyalty, and pleasure. Sex outside of marriage does not bring this level of intimacy. You are kidding yourself if you believe that it does. As it is written:

> Indeed, let God be true but every man a liar.
> —ROMANS 3:4

Have you ever read the Song of Solomon in your Bible? If not, please do so. I think you will consider it quite a treat! There is a verse that is repeated more than once: "Do not stir up nor awaken love Until it pleases" (Song of Sol. 2:7). Pleases who? God! And God is not pleased and never meant for us to awaken those things until the proper time.

14

We should not have sex when we're single—period! Someone has to say it.

Some of you may be thinking, *Who is she to try and tell me how to live my life?* Well, let me tell you something: God is trying to get your attention so that He can bring you into your true purpose. His desire is to have such an impact on your life that whatever your hands touch will surely prosper. But He can only do that with "clean hands." I am simply trying to help you avoid making some of the costly mistakes I made while I was searching for the truth. It took years to remove the debris and traces of all that garbage that polluted my mind and made me think much less of myself than who I was created to be! God created us to be kings and queens—*royalty!* Don't think of yourself as anything less! When this revelation finally kicked in, it literally changed my life. God is speaking to you. He wants to heal you once and for all. But you have to let some of your *flesh* die once and for all. And let me say this again, I am not trying to place condemnation on anyone. It is not my place to judge, nor am I qualified.

There is good news! God, in all of His glory, is ready to forgive you, ready to cleanse you, and ready to redeem you. His love for you is like no other. You can meet Him right where you are and be changed forever. It is never too late! He does not care how far you've strayed or what you've done. If you are in need of forgiveness, He is waiting! If His Spirit is tugging at your heart right now, don't miss this opportunity to be forgiven, healed, and restored.

> If we confess our sins, He is faithful and just to for-
> give us our sins and to cleanse us from all unrigh-
> teousness.
>   —1 John 1:9

Now is the time to surrender to the Lord. Let Him have His way. This is your life-changing moment! If God is speaking to you right now, you can pick this book back up later, but for now, put it down and talk to God! I believe He's waiting.

God revealed to me that there are many single people dying on the vine. I'm talking about in the church. God's Word says:

> God shall judge the righteous and the wicked.
>   —Ecclesiastes 3:17

God always deals with the righteous, the body of Christ, first. There is order in all things with God.

> And you He made alive, who were dead in
> trespasses and sins, in which you once walked
> according to the course of this world…we all
> once conducted ourselves in the lusts of our
> flesh, fulfilling the desires of the flesh and of the
> mind, and were by nature children of wrath, just
> as the others.
>   —Ephesians 2:1–3

> But God, who is rich in mercy, because of His
> great love with which He loved us, even when we

> were dead in trespasses, made us alive together
> with Christ...and raised us up together, and
> made us sit together in the heavenly places in
> Christ Jesus.
>
> —EPHESIANS 2:4–6

When we accept Jesus as Lord and Savior, we are instantly made to sit with Him "in heavenly places." Glory to God! That's why we are expected to live in a manner that exalts the name of Jesus. When we become part of the body of Christ, we are called to higher standards than those who do not yet know Him as Lord and Savior. There is a mandate for us to be the "light of the world" (Matt. 5:14).

> Now, therefore, you are no longer strangers and
> foreigners, but fellow citizens with the saints and
> members of the household of God.
>
> —EPHESIANS 2:19

> I beseech you therefore, brethren, by the mercies of
> God, that you present your bodies a living sacrifice,
> holy, acceptable to God, which is your reasonable
> service.
>
> —ROMANS 12:1

> And I, if I am lifted up from the earth, will draw all
> peoples to Myself.
>
> —JOHN 12:32

How in the world do you think you are lifting up the name of Jesus when you are living loose, living *single*, and having sex, and calling yourself saved? Make no mistake about it; God is calling you to heed His Word. Listen up, *saints!* Jesus is coming back soon. God is calling us to a higher place, because He loves us and wants us healed, transformed, and blessed, so we can be about our Father's business and start being a blessing to others. There are thousands upon thousands of people who need salvation, and there is not much time left.

Jesus said:

> Arise, take up your bed, and go to your house.
> —MATTHEW 9:6

Here is my translation: "Arise, get out of his/her bed, and get back to the house of worship in order to be made whole!" Don't write me any letters! God gave me His permission to say that. As a matter of fact, I heard Him chuckle and say, "You go girl!" That's the kind of relationship I have with my Father.

Please don't leave me now. There is so much more to come. But before we venture on, don't ever forget that there is not one *single* sin God won't forgive! He loves you that much.

THE *SINGLE* MOST IMPORTANT DECISION YOU WILL EVER MAKE

For those who are not yet part of the body of Christ, this is for you. It wouldn't hurt the "church folk" to read this also. First, excuse those of us in the church who may have caused you to distance yourself (because of our ungodly behavior) from the gospel of Jesus Christ. Trust me, we're getting better. We're still being perfected in this walk with God. But whatever you do, don't let that stop you from taking your rightful place in the kingdom. You are following God, not man. Your very livelihood depends on making the next move and taking the next step. *It is without a doubt the single most important decision you will ever make!*

If you've read this far, God has your attention and at this very moment, you can ask God to come into your life. All you need to do is confess your sins and acknowledge that Jesus Christ is Lord of *all* and paid the price by dying on the cross. Finally, believe that He was resurrected from the dead and the blood He shed was for the cleansing of your sin.

> If you confess with your mouth the Lord Jesus and believe in your heart that God has raised Him from the dead, you will be saved. For with the heart one believes unto righteousness, and with the mouth confession is made unto salvation.
>
> —ROMANS 10:9–10

Ask Him to come into your heart and transform every aspect of your life. Surrender completely to Jesus, and you will never be the same. You need to find a local church that preaches the gospel of Jesus Christ. That's where you will get the necessary tools to start your journey. Begin reading the Word of God, the Holy Bible. The Book of

John is a great place to start. Ask God for guidance and "He shall direct your paths" (Prov. 3:6). But the *single* most important piece of advice I can give you to start you on your way is to make God your first love.

Your Invitation From the King

I've chosen you, singled you out
In spite of what you're all about

There's not one sin I won't forgive
I paid the debt so you might live

Just call upon My holy name
And you will never be the same

When you believe within your heart
You'll see the transformation start

My cleansing blood will make you free
And one day soon you'll reign with Me

I will perfect you day by day
I am the Potter, you're the clay

Follow Me and truth you'll find
Feed on My Word, renew your mind

Receive the grace I'm offering
Your invitation from the King

—Deborah J. Griffin

Chapter 2

Your First Love

I F I COULD go back in time and do this thing called *life* all over again, I would have made Jesus Christ my first love. But like so many of us, I was enticed by the lusts of this world and never really understood the benefits of knowing my Creator. Had I known then what I know now, I would have been saved from countless wrong choices, and more importantly, wrong feelings about who I am.

What I'm about to share is probably more relevant for those who are still searching for a true purpose in life. But even if you truly have an understanding of who you are and why you are here, I believe God will speak to you also.

Many of us are aware that:

> God created man in His own image; in the image of God He created him; male and female He created them.
>
> —GENESIS 1:27

But even though we've heard or read this truth, we have not embedded it in our hearts and minds to the point where it has caused us to see ourselves the way God sees us. God created man to have dominion over *all* the earth. It's in your Bible.

> Then God saw everything that He had made, and indeed it was very good.
>
> —GENESIS 1:31

I can't stress this point enough, because it is the true foundation upon which everything else will be built from this point on. God created day and night, the heavens and the earth, the waters and the dry land, the fish of the sea, the birds of the air, and every creeping thing that moved on the earth. But when He created man, He created him in His own image and likeness, and He gave man dominion over all. This, my friend, is truth. Do not be deceived by claims that somehow the earth and everything in it was formed by chance or by some unexplainable cosmic boom. And further more, do not fall into the snare that gives any credence to the tales of evolution. It's simply not true. I have been called to lay the foundation of truth. God has given us another Helper, called the *Holy Spirit*, who will awaken your spirit to this truth. That is not my job, nor am I qualified.

There are two very important principles that need to be established and settled in your mind before we can begin to understand and appreciate how important it is that God should be our first love.

The first principle is that God is omnipotent and Creator of the entire universe—period! He is the beginning and the end. He is King of kings and Lord of lords. He is the great I AM. He is Jehovah. He is God Most High. He is Prince of Peace! (See Exod. 3:14; Ps. 83:18; Isa. 9:6; Rev. 19:16.)

Once you get a glimpse of His infinite wisdom, power, glory, grace, and tender mercies, you will begin to submit to His supremacy and let Him reign in your life. When you truly comprehend the nature of God and understand you were created in His image, you can't help but make Him your first love.

We could stop right here, but there is another principle that needs to be disclosed. When God gave Moses the Ten Commandments, the very first one was:

> You shall have no other gods before Me.
> —Exodus 20:3

The very fact that the Creator of the universe commands us to put Him first is a truth that should not be ignored. We are called to make God our first love.

> You shall love the Lord your God with all your heart, with all your soul, and with all your strength.
> —Deuteronomy 6:5

Check this out! God not only wants you to make Him your first love, but He wants to make you His first love too! And this we all know:

24

> For God so loved the world that He gave His only
> begotten Son, that whoever believes in Him should
> not perish but have everlasting life.
>
> —John 3:16

When this truth penetrated to the deepest parts of my innermost being, I removed all the boundaries and limits I had placed around God and around me. I hope this is helping you. It is my sincere desire that you take hold of this truth for yourself so that God can move in your life and give you the *desires of your heart*. More importantly, He wants to move you into your true purpose. He is doing it for me, and He will do it for you!

> Seek first the kingdom of God and His righteousness, and all these things shall be added to you.
>
> —Matthew 6:33

So how do we make God our first love? I'm so glad you asked! I am going to do my very best to articulate the things that will please God and help you demonstrate your love for Him. But first, let me say this: I am daily being captivated by new levels of His glory, and because of that, it is impossible for me to put together such an exhaustive list. I'm still learning how to show Him my love, and I believe that process will continue to evolve until Jesus Christ comes back. You do know He's coming back, don't you? Just in case there is any doubt in your mind, let me remove it now. Jesus is coming back. And that's a fact. God told me to tell you. You had better listen!

Now back to how we can make God our first love. You need to enter into a relationship with God for yourself before you can even begin that wonderful journey. And it is a process called surrendering to God. As you surrender yourself to Him daily and give Him total lordship over your life, you will begin to hunger and thirst for His presence. He will visit you through His Word, the Holy Bible, while you are in prayer, when you praise and worship Him for who He is, and while you are being ministered to by His anointed disciples.

> And He Himself gave some to be apostles, some prophets, some evangelists, and some pastors and teachers, for the equipping of the saints for the work of ministry, for the edifying of the body of Christ.
>
> —Ephesians 4:11–12

There are a host of other resources (books, tapes, seminars) that will strengthen your walk with God. Ask Him.

> Ask, and it will be given to you; seek, and you will find.
>
> —Matthew 7:7

God's Word is true. If you seek Him, you will find Him. When you find Him, you will love Him.

This is the first step in our journey. Once we begin to submit, God begins to renew, restore, heal, revive, and so much more. His ultimate goal is to make us whole and bring us back to what He created us to be. God made us to love and to worship Him. Now God can begin using you for His glory. He can put you to work to help advance His kingdom. Trust me. There is nothing else in or on this earth that will give you the satisfaction, gratification, fulfillment, completion, and joy that you will receive when you are operating in your true purpose that is orchestrated by the risen King. I hope this is a blessing to you.

HE'S COMING BACK

The Creator of the universe is coming back again,
Though no one knows the day or time,
   we're sensing things will end

Rumors of war, natures travail
   seem evident and clear,
Take heed my friend, the Lord of hosts'
   return is very near

And don't be fooled by lessons taught
   that suggest a cosmic boom
Caused all you see and you to be
   birthed from your mother's womb

Or even tales of long ago that nature played a role,
That man evolved from something less
   and somehow was made whole

The King of kings and Lord of lords
   holds all things in His hand,
And there's a day that's coming soon,
   before Him all will stand

Each knee will bow and tongue confess
   the Word of God is true,
Because of His amazing grace,
   He's speaking now to you

Don't be deceived, He's coming back
   with glory and with power
No man can claim to know the year,
   the day, or exact hour

So when you hear the Master's call,
   receive Him…don't delay!
Get on your knees, say you believe…
   then worship Him and pray.

—DEBORAH J. GRIFFIN

Chapter 3

One Can Put a Thousand to Flight

MOST WHO ARE familiar with this expression equate it to the perils of war. However, God allowed me to see fresh insight and meaning behind this phrase. He began to give me a vision of people literally "soaring" to new heights, new levels of self-worth, and new understandings of who He created us to be. He created us to live above and not below—above our circumstance, above the challenges we face in life, and above the negativity that somehow causes us to lose sight of who we are.

> And the LORD will make you the head and not the tail; you shall be above only, and not be beneath.
> —DEUTERONOMY 28:13

Remember, we are seated in heavenly places when we allow Jesus to rule and reign in our lives. We are seated above with Jesus, who is our chief Intercessor. Don't ever forget that. God's Word declares it!

God also showed me that we are the ones who can catapult (put) people into flight. In other words, we can cause at least a thousand to soar! I'm reminded of that song, *I Believe I Can Fly*.

You may be thinking, *Now wait a minute! How could I possibly cause one thousand people to do anything?* Before I write one more word, remember, "With God all things are possible" (Matt. 19:26). Having said that, most of us will come into contact with at least one thousand people over the course of our lifetime—our children, grandchildren, husband, wife, nephews, nieces, uncles, aunts, parents, grandparents, coworkers, friends, neighbors, and so on. By now, I think you get my point.

Now imagine if all the people we have daily contact with saw the *Jesus* in us. How about a kind word, a word of encouragement, and a sincere smile?

Do you have any idea how we would impact the world? And this is something each and every one of us can do daily. It's such a small thing with such a huge payoff.

I remember once when I was in an elevator and there was a gentleman standing beside me who was dressed very nicely. I admired how well-groomed he was. At first, I hesitated, but then I finally said, "I hope you don't mind me saying this, but you look great—your suit, tie, shoes. You really have it together." His response absolutely amazed me. He looked at me with the biggest smile on his face and said, "You have no idea how much I needed to hear that! Thank you!" At that moment the elevator door opened and he stepped out looking as though he was on top of the world. I believe those few words spoken to him changed his outlook for the entire day. He was soaring, and guess what? That look on his face made me soar too! God is so awesome. When we bless someone, we get blessed right back.

> The generous soul will be made rich, And he who waters will also be watered himself.
>
> —PROVERBS 11:25

God wants us to build up and encourage one another, and in return, we ourselves are edified. God is pleased when we speak words to uplift, inspire, and stir up those around us.

> Death and life are in the power of the tongue.
>
> —PROVERBS 18:21

The very words we speak can act as catalysts to allow others to become more receptive to the gospel of Jesus Christ. Jesus commands us to love one another. In loving one another, did you know that each one of us has the ability to cause others to soar? With God on our side, each one can put a thousand to flight (see Deut. 32:30). It may sound incomprehensible, but it really is not that far out of our reach. If we believe that God will place people in our path that are open to seeing the *Jesus* in us, He will make it happen. But when He does, please make sure that there is some *Jesus* in you to see. And remember:

31

> If God is for us, who can be against us?
>
> —ROMANS 8:31

Starting today, I'm challenging myself to speak words that produce life! Will you step out in faith with me?

THE WORDS YOU SPEAK

Be very careful about what you say
The words you speak will mark your way

I've often wondered if what lies ahead
Is a direct result of something I've said

God's promise to us is everlasting love
And all of His blessings that come from above

Speak of those things that produce life
Not words that lead to needless strife

Choose this day what words to confess
Speak of those things that cause God to bless

The words you speak can kill and destroy
Or what you say will bring forth joy

What words will you choose to speak this day?
Be very careful about what you say.

—DEBORAH J. GRIFFIN

Chapter 4

Be Ye Equally Yoked

Do not be unequally yoked together with
unbelievers.

—2 Corinthians 6:14

God has called us to consider who we connect or join
ourselves to. This fundamental truth is something we
should seriously address if we have a desire to marry and
open our heart to a life-long *relationship*.

Satan would love to use your relationship to interfere
with the plan and purpose God has for your life. Many
people have made the mistake of confusing lust with love.
Or perhaps they have committed themselves to someone
else out of some sense of obligation or even worse, simply
because they were lonely. As a result, divorce rates are at
an all-time high, even within the body of Christ.

One of the reasons it is so important to make God your
first love (*first*) is so that He can bring you into a position
of wholeness and bless you with a good thing. We'll talk
more about that in the sixth chapter of this book.

It is vital to know Him first so that you can be led to the
like-minded individual that will enhance your relationship

with Christ. None of us are perfect, and we should never go into a relationship expecting the other person to complete us. Nor should we marry, expecting to mold that person into what we want him or her to be. Our mates should complement us and help bring out the best in us! Only God can complete us. *God is the Potter; we are the clay!*

When we walk with God and progressively move toward a more intimate relationship with Him, it gives Him pleasure to order our steps.

> The steps of a good man are ordered by the LORD,
> And He delights in his way.
>
> —PSALM 37:23

Along the way, God gives discernment about the type of individual we should want to establish a closer relationship with. His desire is for you to recognize the blessing that He has for you. See yourself as God sees you and believe that you deserve what God wants to give you. Don't settle for anything less!

The relationship you have with God is the foundation on which you will build all future relationships. Next to your relationship with Christ, marriage is the most significant one of all. Marriage is a covenant that is not to be taken lightly. Before you enter into such a long-term commitment, there are certain matters that you need to settle in advance.

I've often heard of disputes between husbands and wives regarding their beliefs about tithing. Tithing is a covenant principle that charges us to give a tenth of our income to the kingdom for the advancement of the gospel of Jesus Christ. You need to have clarity about these types of issues, as well as others, *before* you are joined to someone who does not share the same viewpoint. And just for the record, anyone who is hesitant to tithe to the Lord is missing out on one of God's utmost promises to:

> Pour out for you such blessing
> That there will not be room enough to receive it.
> —MALACHI 3:10

I'm a living witness! This kingdom promise is true. And it's not all about money. He will supply your need, not your greed!

It is vital to have discussions with one another about your beliefs, expectations, and where you are in your walk with God. You need to talk about the plans, purpose, vision, and promises God has put on your heart. And if you are truly walking with God, He will have placed *something* on your heart. If you fail to disclose these truths before you make that decision to marry, you will be setting yourself up for serious disappointment and regret later in your marriage. Do not make that mistake. I'm not saying that you will enter your marriage in full agreement on every aspect of your life. If you're expecting that, you will probably never marry. God created us as individuals. We are not clones. But it is crucial to talk about the most significant relationship you already have—the one with your heavenly *Father*. I'm so glad that I have taken a hold of this truth now, in my *singleness.* If you are single and desire to be married, I hope you grab it too!

So whether your desire is to marry or for restoration in your marriage, let Christ help you first *be equally yoked* to the things of God and then *be equally yoked* with your mate. In other words, make God your first love and your next love (husband/wife) will be supernatural. Please get this in your head; that's what God wants for you. I, for one, am expecting and believing that promise. God's Word is true:

> Therefore I say to you, whatever things you ask when you pray, believe that you receive them, and you will have them.
>
> —MARK 11:24

SEEDTIME AND HARVEST

The Lord has given me seed to sow
And the measure of faith to expect it to grow

His seed that I planted, He allowed to keep growing
For He knew from the harvest, I would keep sowing

The law of seedtime and harvest is true
I'm a living witness of what God will do

The blessings I've received obeying His Word
Are greater than what eyes have seen
   or what ears have heard

Now out of my abundance I sow to reap
Understanding my blessing goes
   beyond what I keep

The fruit of my labor is not all my own
The more I release…the more it has grown

Lord, it's by your grace I'll continue to give
For this is one purpose I'm called to live

I'll gladly go with those you send
I'll cheerfully help bring lack to an end

Use me to release your seed
Use me to supply the need

And never let me stop confessing
How much I want to be a blessing.

—DEBORAH J. GRIFFIN

Chapter 5

The Wedding Gift

UNTIL YOU COME under the lordship of Jesus Christ, many of the principles and truths in the kingdom of heaven will be utter nonsense.

For the message of the cross is foolishness to those who are perishing, but to us who are being saved it is the power of God.

—1 CORINTHIANS 1:18

God has chosen the foolish things of the world to put to shame the wise.

—1 CORINTHIANS 1:27

The Bible declares that the last shall be first, and the first shall be last (Mark 10:31). Give and you shall receive (Luke 6:38). Love your enemy (Luke 6:35). Let the weak say they are strong (Joel 3:10). Let the poor say they are rich. In the natural realm, these truths may seem hard to grasp. The Bible also contains many parables, stories with hidden or symbolic meanings, to make comparisons about the world we live in and the kingdom of heaven. In Matthew 16:25, Jesus declared a very profound truth that explained His eternal promise, a life ruling and reigning with Him:

> For whoever desires to save his life will lose it, but whoever loses his life for My sake will find it.

Keeping in line with this same doctrine, God began to shed light on a precious *gift* He has made available to you and me.

Anyone who has attended a wedding will most likely agree that it is usually the custom of the bride and groom to open their gifts either at the end of the ceremony, or at some other point in time when all the guests have gone home. But God, in His infinite wisdom, began to show me that the *gift* He has for us is for our enjoyment and edification *before* the wedding takes place. The gift is the Holy Spirit, and He wants you to have this indwelling before you get married, so that you can be led by the Spirit of God, and not by your flesh, when you are seeking your mate!

When Jesus Christ died on the cross, the debt was paid once and for all. His was the final sacrifice for the forgiveness of sin for all mankind. And when He was resurrected and seated next to the Father, He sent us a Comforter or Helper, called the Holy Spirit! This precious gift was sent to build us up, help us to discern the truth, give revelation of His Word, and to ultimately empower us to walk not according to the *flesh*, but according to the *spirit*. The Holy Spirit is our Teacher, Helper, and Guide. The amazing thing is that if we want this gift, all we have to do is ask. God is good!

> If you then, being evil, know how to give good gifts to your children, how much more will your heavenly Father give the Holy Spirit to those who ask Him!
>
> —LUKE 11:13

After searching Scripture for further understanding about the Holy Spirit and other spiritual gifts, I whole-heartedly believe that we need this infilling to operate in the capacity that will enable God's best to flow through us.

> But the Helper, the Holy Spirit, whom the Father will send in My name, He will teach you all things, and bring to your remembrance all things that I said to you.
>
> —JOHN 14:26

> Likewise the Spirit also helps in our weaknesses. For we do not know what we should pray for as we ought, but the Spirit Himself makes intercession for us with groanings which cannot be uttered.
>
> —ROMANS 8:26

> But you shall receive power when the Holy Spirit has come upon you.
>
> —ACTS 1:8

> And they were all filled with the Holy Spirit and
> began to speak with other tongues, as the Spirit
> gave them utterance.
>
> —ACTS 2:4

We need to ask for this gift while we are single. Our desire should be to say, "I do," to the infilling of the Holy Spirit before we are married. If we have a sincere longing to follow Christ and make Him Lord of all, we need to understand the importance of relying on the Holy Spirit to help us live a victorious life!

ABCs of a Victorious Life

Ask for the infilling of the Holy Spirit
Be steadfast and unmovable
Cast your cares upon the Lord
Do not forsake the assembly of God
Encourage one another
Forgive others as God forgives you
Give and it shall be given unto you
Humble yourself before God and man
Intimacy with God is essential
Jesus is the truth and the way
Keep His Word hidden in your heart
Love one another
Meditate on God's Word
Never give up
Offer your body as a living sacrifice
Pray for wisdom and understanding
Quiet time before the Lord is transforming
Resist the devil and he will flee
Seek ye first the kingdom of God
Trust Him at all times
Use the whole armor of God
Vision will keep you from stumbling
Worship the Lord
Expect to hear from God
You are a child of the Most High God
Zeal ignites purpose and victory

—Deborah J. Griffin

Chapter 6

Two Can Put Ten Thousand to Flight

He who finds a wife finds a good thing,
And obtains favor from the LORD.

—PROVERBS 18:22

Now this is for all the men out there! Listen very carefully. You are highly favored when the woman you marry is a good thing because *all* good things come from God.

And, ladies, this is for you! When you marry a man who walks in the favor of God because you are his good thing, the two of you are unstoppable. Need I say more? Let's stop right here and SHOUT!

One of the ways to identify whether or not you are yoked to a good thing is by observing the character and lifestyle of your future mate.

> But the fruit of the Spirit is love, joy, peace, longsuffering, kindness, goodness, faithfulness, gentleness, self-control.
>
> —GALATIANS 5:22–23

> Add to your faith virtue, to virtue knowledge, to knowledge self-control, to self-control perseverance, to perseverance godliness, to godliness brotherly kindness, and to brotherly kindness love. For if these things are yours and abound, you will be neither barren nor unfruitful in the knowledge of our Lord Jesus Christ.
>
> —2 PETER 1:5–8

Two equally yoked, sold out to Jesus, Holy Spirit-filled, foot-stomping, hand-clapping, prayerfully seeking, purpose-driven, vision-loaded individuals can put ten thousand to flight. Can I get an Amen?

God began to show me how the type of married couple I just described can enter a place where He will use them to a degree that is truly limitless. If you allow God to be as BIG as He is, He will literally enlarge your territory and increase your vision ten thousand fold. Remember, He is a BIG God if we take the boundaries off. He will be as BIG as you allow Him to be!

When I began to let God be BIG in my life, my vision was enhanced and my spirit was stirred like never before. And it is not over yet, there's still so much more He plans to do. I get excited just thinking about what He has in store for me. I hope you are excited too!

> My soul, wait silently for God alone, For my expectation is from Him.
>
> —PSALM 62:5

Always remember God's promise to us:

> Again I say to you that if two of you agree on earth
> concerning anything that they ask, it will be done
> for them by My Father in heaven.
>
> —Matthew 18:19

When the Lord blesses us with that special mate with whom we will spend the rest of our life, I believe He has much more in store for us than just saying, "I do." He ultimately wants to take us to a place that produces such fruit and such a bountiful harvest that, in the end, He will say, "Well done, My good and faithful servant. Well done!" (Matt. 25:21, author's paraphrase).

WELL DONE

You've fasted, you've prayed and stayed up at night,
Meditated on My Word and fought the good fight

When the dawn was yet breaking
   you fed on My Word
The prompting of My Spirit you faithfully heard

Don't be discouraged, it won't be much longer
Continue your path, each step you grow stronger

The season is coming when the race that you've run,
Will bring untold blessings for all you have done

Don't be disheartened for my promise is sure,
I've seen you stand…watched you endure

Your hope in the gospel is certain, my son,
My good and faithful servant, well done…
   well done!

—DEBORAH J. GRIFFIN

Afterword

I HOPE YOU HAVE enjoyed our journey together and that you were blessed by reading this book (as much as I was while writing it).

Next to accepting Jesus Christ as my Lord and Savior, this was unquestionably one of the most amazing and life-changing experiences I have ever encountered.

My prayer and desire is that you are transformed too! From this day forward, grab hold of your true destiny, your true purpose, and your eternal promise!

> That you may walk worthy of the Lord, fully pleasing Him, being fruitful in every good work and increasing in the knowledge of God.
>
> —COLOSSIANS 1:10

Whatever you do, do not miss out on one *single* thing God has for you!

And remember, if your desire is to marry in God's perfect timing, then enjoy being single for this season until you marry for the right reason!

To Contact the Author

Deborah J. Griffin
BeFruitFul.biz
6805 W. Commercial Blvd., #322
Tamarac, FL 33319

Toll free number: (888) 9SAVIOR

E-mail: Deborah@BeFruitFul.biz.

Web site: www.BeFruitFul.biz.

BeFruitFul.biz™
"About My Father's Business"

...ingle for a Season, Married a long-overdue resource for "singles." She skillfully ...ny, poetry, and timeless truths of Scripture into a ...spiration, counsel, and guidance (ultimately the basis for a healthy Christian marriage). A must-read!

—CHARLES H. WILLIAMS
PASTOR, GRACE CHAPEL, INGLEWOOD, CALIFORNIA

The Lord is singling you out for total transformation!

According to author Deborah Griffin, if you are single, you are not alone, but "singled-out" for an especially intimate relationship with the Lord! You're invited to…

- View the single person's life through God's eyes.
- Live a fulfilling—rather than lonely—daily life in the presence of the Lord.
- Rejoice in Jesus Christ and be blessed and completely transformed.

If you are single with a desire to one day marry, you don't want to miss the life-changing truth revealed in this book. And even if you're not single, you will be blessed, too! *Single for a Season, Married for a Reason* contains an underlying message for the church and everyone on planet Earth who is searching for a better life, a better future, and more importantly, an eternal promise.

Deborah Griffin has spoken at women's retreats and ministered in small group, Bible study, and prayer group settings at different churches in the Los Angeles area. After recently retiring from a twenty-one-year career in advertising sales for *The Wall Street Journal*, she resides in Florida with her daughter.

CREATION HOUSE
A STRANG COMPANY

Christian Living/Relationships/
Single Living

ISBN-10: 1-59979-092-0
ISBN-13: 978-1-59979-092-3

50699

9 781599 790923

$6.99

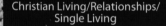